Beijing: Glimpses of History

北 京 揽 胜

北京揽胜

外文出版社　北京

Beijing: Glimpses of History

FOREIGN LANGUAGES PRESS   BEIJING

Editor: Liao Pin
English text by: Arnold Chao (Zhao Yihe)
Photographs by:
Hu Chui Hu Weibiao Xing Yansheng
Huang Taopeng Jiang Jingyu Sun Shuqing
He Bingfu Liu Shizhao Liu Wenmin
Sun Shuming Sun Yongxue Liu Chungen
Yu Tianwei Niu Songlin Hu Baoyu
Zhou Youma Liu Chen Xie Jun
Yan Zhongyi Meng Zi Yang Yin
Gu Weiheng Jin Yaowen Gao Mingyi
Wang Zhengbao Wei Mingxiang and others
Designer Li Shiji

编　辑　　廖　頻
翻　譯　　趙一鶴
攝　影　　胡　錘　胡維標　邢延生　黃韜鵬
　　　　　姜景餘　孫樹清　何炳富　劉世昭
　　　　　劉文敏　孫樹明　孫永學　王正保
　　　　　劉春根　于天爲　牛嵩林　胡寶玉
　　　　　周幼馬　劉　臣　謝　軍　嚴鍾義
　　　　　蒙　紫　楊　茵　谷維恒　金耀文
　　　　　高明義　魏銘祥等
裝幀設計　　李士伋

First Edition 1989
Second Printing 1992
Third Printing 1993
Fourth Printing 1994
ISBN 0-8351-2329-4
ISBN 7-119-00735-1

Copyright 1989 by Foreign Languages Press, Beijing, China

Published by Foreign Languages Press
24 Baiwanzhuang Road, Beijing 100037, China

Distributed by China International Book Trading Corporation
35 Chegongzhuang Xilu, Beijing 100044, China
P.O. Box 399, Beijing, China

Printed in the People's Republic of China

Contents

With the Forbidden City lying contiguous to former imperial gardens like the North Sea, the Central Sea and the South Sea, the halls and pavilions, towers and pagodas in central Beijing lend their charm to one another at night, reminding one of the heavenly palaces of gods in oriental fairy tales. The picture shows a watchtower on the wall of the Forbidden City on the left, the Pavilion of Ten Thousand spring Seasons on Prospect Hill on the right, and the White Dagoba in the North Sea in the distance.

古城之夜。市區中部，紫禁城與北海、景山、中南海等皇家苑園毗連，殿閣塔亭交相輝映，使人聯想起東方的神宮仙宇。圖中右為景山頂峯的萬春亭，左為紫禁城角樓，遠處為北海的白塔。

A History of 3,000 Years
—In lieu of Introduction

by *Zhao Luo**

The earliest record of Beijing identifies the city as "Ji", which means "thistle", a weedy plant with prickly leaves and purplish flowers. In the 11th century B.C. Ji was a vassal state of the Western Zhou Dynasty (c. 11th century–771 B.C.). In the ensuing period known as Spring and Autumn (770–476 B.C.), Ji was annexed by its formidable neighbour, Yan, another vassal state of Western Zhou located to the southwest of Ji. The city of Ji served as the capital for the state of Yan until 226 B.C., when Yan was conquered by the powerful state of Qin which unified the whole of China five years later. Archaeologists point out that the site of the ancient city of Ji lies most probably in the southwest suburbs of present-day Beijing.

The city acquired ever greater importance as one dynasty replaced another. Starting as the capital of an ancient vassal state, it eventually became the national capital of a great empire. This evolution can be explained by many factors, and one of them is geographical.

Located in the northwest corner of the North China Plain, Beijing is protected by mountains on the north, the east and the west. To the south lies the extensive North China Plain. Goegraphers liken the big plain to

*The author of this article is Senior Editor and Editor-in-Chief of the Beijing Publishing House for Ancient Classices.—Ed.

a sea and the small plain around Beijing to a gulf. The mountains on three sides of Beijing separate it from the Mongolia Plateau and the Northeast China Plain. In the old times these mountains served as natural barriers for the dynastic rulers of the Han Chinese to resist invasion by nomadic peoples from the north. However, the high and precipitous mountains have never been closed barriers. You can travel through them if you know how to use the zigzag and intertwined trails. An important mountain pass to the northeast of Beijing, known as Gubeikou, leads to the Northeast China Plain. Another one, lying to the northwest of the city and called Guangou, connects with the Mongolia Plateau. In peacetime the mountain passes and trails are used by merchants travelling between north and south. In wartime they acquire a strategic significance and become vital to the contestants.

For over 1,000 years, therefore, the city of Ji remained an important military stronghold and trade centre in North China in spite of more than a dozen dynastic changes. This was the situation from 221 B.C., the year of the founding of Qin, the first feudal empire with centralized power in China's history, to the 10th century. During this period, the city was known as Zhuojun or Youzhou at different times, depending on the name of the region for which it served as the capital city.

In 938 the city of Ji was made the secondary capital of the Liao Dynasty founded by the Khitan people, an ethnic minority which had built up its power in Northeast China. It was also called the Southern Capital because of its location in the southern part of Liao territory. Under the Liao, the city acquired for the first time the name of Yanjing, which is still being used in the names of many commercial and other establishments in Beijing today.

More than a century later, the Jurchens, another ethnic minority in China, founded the Jin Dynasty, vanquished Liao, moved their capital to Yanjing in 1153, and renamed it Middle Capital. In 1214, under the attacks of the powerful Mongol army, the rulers of Jin moved their capital to Bianjing, i.e., Kaifeng in present-day Henan. The next year the Middle Capital of the Jin Dynasty fell under the iron hoofs of the Mongol cavalry.

In 1267 the Mongol ruler, Kublai Khan, gave orders for the construction of a new city to the northeast of the Middle Capital of the Jin Dynasty. Four years later, he ascended the throne and founded the Yuan Dynasty (1271-1368) in the new capital which was still under construction. The project was completed in 1285. Given the name of Dadu (Great Capital), the city was described as "matchless in the world" by Marco Polo in his *Travels*. By then Beijing had replaced the other historical capital cities, including Chang'an, Luoyang and Bianliang, as China's political centre, a position it retained through two more dynasties, the Ming (1368-1644) and the Qing (1644-1911).

A republican revolution broke out on October 10, 1911, forcing the Qing emperor to abdicate in February the next year. This marked the collapse of the last feudal dynasty in China and also the end of Beijing's history as the imperial capital. The next thirty years and more witnessed the city's ordeal—harassment in the incessant wars among warlords, eight years of Japanese occupation from 1937 to 1945, and a return to Kuomintang rule in 1945.

On January 31, 1949, the peaceful liberation of the city was achieved by the People's Liberation Army through negotiations with the Kuomintang garrison authorities. On October 1 the same year, the founding of the People's Republic of China was announced from the gatetower of Tiananmen (the Gate of Heavenly Peace), and Beijing became its capital.

Today's Beijing has taken on many modern features. Increasing contact with the outside world and rapid commercialization of the economy in the past decade have resulted in the appearance of blocks of high rises, overpasses and ring roads, the last being the prototype of freeways. Some of the historical relics have disappeared in the process, such as most of the old city walls and the gorgeous archways at the intersections of business districts. Foreign visitors, particularly architects, complain against the demolition of these centuries-old structures. Shrugging their shoulders, city planners say that it couldn't be helped because of the need to cope with a growing volume of motor traffic.

In spite of the modern changes, the basic characteristics of the ancient capital are kept intact. Beijing used to be a set of four square cities with one placed inside another: the Outer City, the Inner City, the Imperial City and, finally, the Forbidden City. While the delineation of the first three is hardly visible, the Forbidden City remains what it has always been. From one of the towers in the Forbidden City you can still see the neat layout of old Beijing, with the Ancestral Temple of the royal family placed to the left of the palace complex and the Altar of Land and Grain to its right,* and with the Temple of Heaven in the south of the city, the Temple of Earth in the north, the Altar of the Sun in the east, and the Altar of the Moon in the west. If you take a stroll from your hotel, you may arrive in one of the street alleys lined by old-fashioned square courtyards, the homes of many local citizens. The former imperial gardens both inside and outside the city, the Great Wall snaking along the mountains in the north, the Thirteen Tombs of the Ming Dynasty in the northwest suburbs and the great number of temples and pagodas combine to make Beijing a big museum of history.

In the precent album, we will take you to the best-known historical sites in and around Beijing.

---

*The Ancestral Temple of the royal family has become the Working People's Palace of Culture, and the Altar of Land and Grain, the Sun Yat-sen Park.—*Ed.*

序　篇

趙　洛

在歐亞大陸的東部，有一座四四方方的城。城的四周原來圍以高大堅固的磚砌城牆，四面對稱地開着十六個拱形門洞，門洞之上是飛檐凌空的城樓。立於其上，可以遠眺數十里之外。在城的中央至今仍兀立着一座"城中之城"——紫禁城。紫禁城的周圍是整齊如畦、經緯分明的街巷，兩旁排列着商舖，民居。彎曲的河流，美麗的園苑，莊嚴神幻的古代祭壇和寺廟，錯落其間，使方直中融入了環曲，規整對稱中顯示出變化。這座城便是北京。薊、涿、幽州、南京、燕京、中都、大都、北平，則是它在各個歷史時期的名稱。濃郁的東方色彩，恢宏的氣勢，悠遠的歷史，使這座城具有一種神奇的魅力。一位外國城市規劃專家曾這樣評價過它："地球表面上人類最偉大的作品可能是北京。"

這"人類最偉大的作品"凝集着中華民族文化的精華，是歷代匠師綿延不斷地締造經營而成的。爲這座城市奠定第一塊基石的年代，可追溯到三千多年以前。

北京最早見於文獻的名稱叫做薊。公元前十一世紀時，薊國是統治中國北方的西周王朝的一個分封國。春秋（公元前七七〇年——前四七六年）中期，位於薊國西南面的另一個封國燕，吞併了薊，並遷都於薊城。從這時起，直到公元前二二六年燕國被强大的秦國所滅，薊城一直是燕的都城。**據考古學家考證，當年的薊城就在現北京城區的西南部。**

從薊城誕生到今日的北京，其間儘管朝代屢屢更迭，城名也幾次變換，但是，這座城市却不斷發展、擴大，由偏居一隅的封國都城，躍居爲中國幾代的赫赫帝都。其久盛不衰的重要條件之一就是它所處的優異的地理位置。

北京位於華北大平原的西北角，這平原一角的西、北和東北三面，叢山環抱；南面與之相連的華北平原廣袤平坦，猶如碧波萬頃的海洋。因此，地理學家形象地將北京所在的小平原稱爲"北京灣"。拱衛在"北京灣"三面的莽莽羣山，層巒疊嶂，高峻險要，是橫亘在蒙古高原、東北平原與北京之間的屏障。幾千年以前，這道屏障曾是佔據中原的漢族王朝防衛、抵禦北方游牧民族南下的天然防線。然而這道防線又並非全然封閉，在那崇山峻嶺之中，還有一條條曲曲折折深邃的山谷。其中最重要的兩條是關溝和古北口，它們分別位於北京小平原的西北和東北，經由這兩條峽谷可抵達蒙古高原和東北平原。山間的條條幽谷，平時是南來北往的商旅必經的通道，戰時是敵對雙方攻守的要隘。而北京小平原上的薊城扼南北通道的咽喉，形勢十分險要。因此，自公元前二二一年秦建立中國歷史上第一個中央集權封建王國之後，直至公元十世紀，一千多年間，朝代更易十餘次，但薊城却始終是北方的軍事重鎮和貿易中心。這其間又因它曾先後是涿郡和幽州的治所，所

趙洛　北京古籍出版社總編輯、編審。

以，涿郡和幽州也一度成爲它的名稱。

公元九三八年，薊城成爲遼的陪都。遼是崛起於中國東北方的少數民族契丹人建立的。因爲薊位於它所轄的疆域的南部，所以改稱南京，又叫燕京。一個多世紀以後，另一個少數民族女真人建立的金朝將遼滅亡，並於一一五三年遷都燕京，改名中都。一二一四年，金朝因受到新興的蒙古族軍隊的進攻，被迫遷都汴京（今河南開封），第二年蒙古鐵騎入佔中都。一二六七年，蒙古族首領忽必烈下令在中都城的東北郊築建新城。四年後這位首領即在興建中的都城內登上皇帝的寶座，建立了中國歷史上的元朝。一二八五年新城全部建成，這便是意大利旅行家馬可·波羅在遊記中稱之爲"世界莫能與比"的元大都。從此，北京取代了長安、洛陽、汴梁等古都的地位，成爲中國的政治中心，並延續到明、清兩代。

一九一一年十月十日，中國爆發了資産階級民主主義革命，第二年二月清帝被迫宣告退位。至此，中國最後一個封建王朝潰亡，北京作爲帝都的歷史到此結束。在此後的三十多年里，北京歷經苦難：先是連年不斷的軍閥戰爭，使當年的帝都變得衰微破敗；一九三七年日本侵略軍侵入，古城在血與火中苦熬了八年；抗日戰爭勝利後，國民黨政府接管了這座城市。

苦難、屈辱、血淚，終於使人民起而抗爭。一九四九年十月一日，中華人民共和國成立，北京成爲新生的共和國的首都，古城的歷史揭開新的一頁。

歲月流逝，如今要重睹北京舊時的風貌和曾在這里出現過的那些歷史場景已不可能。但是，當人們置身於它的城區或四野，面對那些觸目皆是的歷史印痕，却感到那悠遠的過去並非無法追尋。一座默默聳立的古塔，往往凝聚着一代藝術的精華；一塊苔蘚斑駁的碑石，或許記載着一件轟動一時的壯舉；面對被焚毀的宮苑廢墟，猶如讀一部屈辱史；登上長城透過它的雉堞望蒼茫羣山，可以想見當年那"烽火連天遠，鐵騎鏖戰急"的景象……北京城像一座宏大的歷史博物館，祇須在這裏作一次巡視，便能直接感觸到這座古城的歷史。

今天的北京是歷史上北京的延續和發展。它的空間佈局依然保留着歷史的印跡，但是，在那雕樑畫棟的古建築羣之間，無數的現代化樓羣拔地而起；古意猶存的街巷與環繞城內外的坦平大道相接；傳统的四合院與新型的住宅區並存……在這裏，過去與現在，歷史與現實，古老的傳統與時代精神交融、凝煉在一起，使這座充滿濃重歷史文化氛圍的古城透出勃勃生機。

一座城市的歷史就是一個國家的歷史。作爲幾代帝都和今日中國首都的北京是中國歷史和現狀的縮影。因此，作一次"北京遊"不僅可以觀賞到一座保留較爲完整的古代京城，而且可以觀察、瞭解中國。

The Palace Complex

宮　闕

The palace complex known as the Forbidden City stands in the centre of Beijing. It is protected by high walls and a moat on all four sides and consists of dozens of halls and courtyards. The emperors of two dynasties, the Ming and the Qing, lived here with their families and hundreds of court ladies and palace eunuchs. From their throne in the Forbidden City they governed the country by holding court sessions with their ministers, issuing imperial edicts and initiating military expeditions. Sometimes they gave oral tests to candidates for the highest academic degrees by asking them questions on the meaning of Confucian classics and soliciting their views on state policies.

In Chinese the palace complex is called Purple Forbidden City. "Purple" doesn't refer to the colour of the buildings or walls, but has a mythological origin. It is said that the Emperor of Heaven has his palaces in the region of the North Star, of which purple is the symbolic colour. The abode of the temporal emperor, therefore, is supposed to have the same colour. The Purple Forbidden City was inaccessible to the common people. Even the highest civil and military officers could not enter it without good reason.

The Forbidden City was completed in 1420 during the Ming Dynasty. It was the home of 24 emperors of the Ming and Qing dynasties. Naturally it was the scene of many important events affecting the course of Chinese history, including political struggles and palace coups, some of them extremely tragic. After the republican revolution of 1911, the last emperor of the Qing Dynasty, then still a child, abdicated the next year. But he and his family and their entire entourage were allowed to stay in the palaces and continued to lead an extravagant life on a huge allowance from the republican government. They were finally expelled by republican troops in 1924. The Forbidden City was renamed the Palace Museum and opened to the general public.

在北京城的中央有一組巍峨雄偉的宮殿羣，四周環繞着高大的牆垣。這便是明清兩代的帝王的宮室紫禁城。

古代神話傳説天帝住紫微垣。人間帝王自詡是天帝之子，古人就把帝王的住所叫做紫宮。皇宮是常人不能進入的禁地，因此，北京的宮城叫紫禁城。

北京紫禁城從公元一四二○年建成到一九二四年中國歷史上最後一個皇帝從宮內被逐出，這裏居住過明清兩代的二十四個皇帝。五百年間，許多影響中國歷史進程、主宰億萬人命運的重大決策都出自這裏；皇室中無數的政治紛爭、權力較量和凄婉哀艷的故事也發生在這裏。所有這一切給這座莊嚴神聖的宮城罩上了一層神秘的色彩。

Panorama of the Forbidden City, which occupies a total space of more than 720,000 square metres. The buildings in this palace complex are measured in 9,999.5 bays. The surrounding palace walls are 10 metres high and have a total length of 3,400 metres, and are protected by a 52-metre-wide moat. The Forbidden City consists of two parts, the Outer Court and the Inner Court. The Outer Court centres around the Hall of Supreme Harmony, the Midway Hall of Harmony and the Hall of Preserved Harmony, which are flanked by the hall of Literary Glory and the Hall of Military Prowess. The Inner Court centres around the Hall of Celestial Purity, the Hall of Union and Peace and the Hall of Terrestrial Tranquility, which are flanked by the Six East Palaces and the Six West Palaces. The layout is orderly and symmetrical. The picture shows the Forbidden City viewed from the north.

被稱爲"殿宇之海"的紫禁城，總面積七十二萬多平方米，有殿宇宮室九千九百九十九間半。周圍環繞着高 米，長三千四百米的宮牆，牆外有五十二米寬的護城河。紫禁城分外朝和內廷兩 份。外朝以太和、中和、保和三大殿爲中心，文華、武英殿爲兩翼；內廷以乾 交泰殿、坤寧宮爲中心，東西六宮爲兩翼，佈局嚴謹有序。圖爲由北向南眺望 。

The tower of the South-Facing Gate. The Forbidden City used to be enclosed by the Imperial City, the Inner City and the Outer City one outside the other. As the main gate on the south side of the Inner City, the South-Facing Gate was designated for exclusive use by the emperor. Built in 1421, it is 42 metres high and stands exactly on the north-south axis of Beijing.

正陽門城樓。紫禁城的外圍依次築有皇城、內城和外城。正陽門是內城的正南門，專供皇帝出入。城樓建於一四二一年，高四十二米，位於全城的南北中軸線上。

The 33.7-metre-high Tiananmen (Gate of Heavenly Peace), the main gate of the Imperial City, was first built in 1417 and rebuilt in 1651. It was used by the emperor for grand ceremonies, for the launching of military expeditions under his personal command, and for his royal wedding. Imperial edicts were issued from the gatetower.

皇城的正門天安門，通高三三點七米，始建於一四一七年，現在的天安門爲一六五一年重建。封建帝王外出舉行重大典禮、親征、迎娶皇后都從此門出入；城樓上是頒發詔令的地方。

With a space of 440,000 square metres, the Tiananmen Square
is an expansion of the square in front the Imperial City.

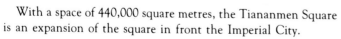
天安門廣場。佔地四十四萬平方米，由舊時的皇宮廣場擴展而成。

This is one of the two ornamental columns in front of the Tiananmen. With carved decorations on the white marble, they were erected when the Forbidden City was being built in the 15th century. Each column weighs 20 tons.

天安門前有一對漢白玉石雕成的華表，每座重兩萬公斤，是十五世紀時與紫禁城同時建造的。

The Meridian Gate as viewed from inside the Forbidden City. Built in 1420, it is 37.95 metres high and is the main gate of the Forbidden City. The bells and drums in the gatetower were sounded to accompany important ceremonies presided over by the emperor.

從紫禁城內望午門。午門是紫禁城的正門，通高三七點九五米，建於一四二〇年。城樓置鐘鼓，每逢皇帝主持大典，鐘鼓齊鳴，以壯聲威。

During important ceremonies presided over by the emperor, guards of honour lined up on the square between the Meridian Gate and the Gate of Supreme Harmony, the largest square in the palace complex.

午門與太和門之間的廣場是皇宮內最大的廣場，皇帝舉行大典時在此排列儀仗。

Built from south to north on an eight-metre-high marble foundation, the Hall of Supreme Harmony, the Midway Hall of Harmony and the Hall of Preserved Harmony form the Outer Court of the Forbidden City together with the Hall of Literary Glory on their east side and the Hall of Military Prowess on their west side.

太和、中和、保和三座大殿由南至北排列在高八米的漢白玉臺基上。它們及其東西兩翼的文華殿、武英殿，組成了紫禁城的外朝。

The Hall of Supreme Harmony, also referred to as the throne, is 35 metres high, the highest of the halls in the Forbidden City. It was used for important ceremonies like the enthronement of the crown prince, the emperor's birthday celebrations, and the initiation of military expeditions.

太和殿。亦稱金鑾殿，是紫禁城內最高大的殿宇，殿高三十五米。皇帝登基、慶賀誕辰、出兵征討等大典都在此舉行。

The Mirror of the Yellow Emperor hangs from the coffered ceiling in the Hall of Supreme Harmony. It is said to have been made by the Yellow Emperor, the first legendary ruler of China, and was enshrined by the emperors from one generation to another as a symbol of the orthodoxy of their rule.

太和殿的蟠龍藻井下倒垂着軒轅寶鏡。軒轅鏡相傳是中國遠古時代軒轅氏黃帝所造。歷代皇帝因襲懸掛，以示自己是正統皇帝。

With carved dragon designs, the emperors throne is placed at the centre of the Hall of Supreme Harmony.

殿內皇帝的雕龍寶座高踞中央，周圍陳設華美。

The Inner Court provided luxurious accommodation for the emperor and his family—the empress, the consorts, the crown prince, the empress dowager, the consorts of the late emperor, etc. Each courtyard, forming an independent division, is complete with a bed chamber, a reception room and side chambers.

殿宇重重的内廷是皇帝、后妃、太子、太后、太妃們的居處。

The courtyards in the Inner Court are linked by roads, at both ends of which are gates and rooms for the guards. The picture shows a long passageway in the Inner Court.

深宮長街。内廷的各組宮殿之間，以縱橫的街巷相聯，街巷的兩端設有宮門和警衛值房。

The three main halls in the Inner Court are the Hall of Celestial Purity, the Hall of Union and Peace, and the Hall of Terrestrial Tranquility. The picture shows the front chamber of the Hall of Celestial Purity, where the emperor attended to state affairs almost everyday.

乾清宮、交泰殿和坤寧宮是內廷的三大殿。乾清宮是皇帝居住和處理日常政務的地方。圖為乾清宮正殿內景。

Lying between the Hall of Celestial Purity and the Hall of Terrestrial Tranquility, the Hall of Union and Peace was used for the safekeeping of 25 jade seals of the imperial court. Representing monarchial authority, they were placed in golden boxes covered with yellow silk.

位於乾清宮與坤寧宮之間的交泰殿，是清代放置寶璽的地方。這裏收藏着二十五方代表皇權的印璽，用金盒盛裝、黄綢覆蓋。

The Hall of Terrestrial Tranquility was the residence of the empress and contained her bed chamber. The picture shows the east side chamber of the hall, which served as the bridal chamber for the emperor and empress during their wedding. As a rule, they stayed here only for three days before returning to their respective residences.

坤寧宮是皇后的寢宮。圖爲坤寧宮東側室，是皇帝大婚時的洞房。大婚時帝后祇在此居住三日，然後回到各自所住的宮內。

Located to the west of the Hall of Celestial Purity and to the south of the Six West Palaces, the Hall of Mental Cultivation served as the residence as well as the office of the emperor in the late period of the Qing Dynasty. Both Emperor Tongzhi (r. 1862-74) and Emperor Guangxu (r. 1875-1908) were enthroned long before they came of age.

All important affairs were referred to Empress Dowager Cixi, mother of Emperor Tongzhi and aunt of Emperor Guangxu. The picture shows the East Chamber of Warmth in the Hall of Mental Cultivation, where Empress Dowager Cixi "ruled the country from behind a curtain". While the child emperor sat on the throne during a court session in this chamber, the Empress Dowager sitting behind a curtain would answer all the questions from the ministers and make all the decisions.

位於乾清宮之西、西六宮南面的養心殿是清代後期皇帝居住和處理日常政務的地方。圖為養心殿東暖閣。同治、光緒兩朝太后曾在這裏"垂簾聽政"。同治、光緒二帝都是幼年登上皇位的，在很長一段時間內，一切政事由同治的母親、光緒的伯母慈禧太后決定。召對羣臣時，小皇帝坐在寶座上，太后坐在紗簾後應答裁定。

A chamber at the western end of the Hall of Mental Cultivation is called the Hall of Three Rarities. This is the place where Emperor Qianlong (r. 1736-95) of the Qing Dynasty kept three copybooks of calligraphic models—one by the ancient master calligrapher Wang Xizhi, another by his son Wang Xianzhi, and a third one by Wang Xun.

養心殿最西面的一間宮室，是以珍藏書法名帖而著名的"三希堂"。

The Hall of Preserved Elegance, one of the Six West Palaces, once served as the residence of Empress Dowager Cixi. The bed with two silk curtains in front is typical of one in a rear chamber in those days.

西六宮之一——儲秀宮。宮內陳設奢侈豪華，牀前懸掛雙重帳幔是典型的後宮寢室形式。慈禧曾在這裏居住過。

Two scenes in the Imperial Garden at the back of the three main halls of the Inner Court. The garden was built in 1417. On the left is the Pavilion of Ten Thousand Spring Seasons, one of the eight pavilions in the middle of the garden. Arranged symmetrically on both sides of the central axis, each two of them follow a single architectural pattern. The other picture shows the Hill of Accumulated Elegance and the pavilion on it in the northeast corner of the garden. On the ninth day of the ninth lunar month every year the Emperor and Empress would ascend the hill to enjoy the scenery in the distance.

御花園中的兩處景致。御花園位於內廷三大殿後，始建於一四一七年。左圖爲園內的萬春亭。御花園中部有八座亭子，造型兩兩相同，左右對稱地分佈在中軸線兩側，萬春亭爲其中之一。上圖爲園東北角的堆秀山，山上築亭，每年農歷九月九日重陽節時，帝后們登臨其上，眺望遠處風光。

The big stage in the Pavilion of Cheerful Melodies in the eastern section of the Forbidden City. With a height of 20.71 metres, the three-storeyed stage was equipped with trap doors for actors to present scenes in heaven, in the human world, and in the nether regions.

紫禁城西部的暢音閣大戲臺，臺高二〇點七一米，分上、中、下三層，演員可以利用滑車升上趨下，表演天上、人間、地下的劇目。

A small stage for theatrical performances in the Studio for Retirement, where Emperor Qianlong lived after he abdicated in favour of the crown prince in 1795.

乾隆花園倦勤齋內的小戲臺。乾隆花園位於紫禁城東部，是清乾隆皇帝晚年頤養的地方。

The north gate of the Imperial Garden viewed at dusk. It leads to the Gate of Divine Might, the rear gate of the Forbidden City.

暮靄中的順貞門。順貞門是御花園的北門，出此門便是紫禁城的後門神武門。

This is one of the watchtowers on the four corners of the wall surrounding the Forbidden City. Each watchtower is supported by nine beams and 18 pillars and has three layers of eaves. There are 72 ridges on the roof with a gilded spire in the centre.

紫禁城垣的四隅，各建有一座角楼。四座角楼造型相同，分别由九梁、十八柱、三重檐、七十二脊构成，楼顶置有鎏金宝顶。

Imperial Gardens

園　林

The imperial gardens in Beijing and its suburbs were bulit as a complement to the Forbidden City. Symbolic of the supremacy of royal power, the Forbidden City had to be given an atmosphere of magnificence and solemnity in architectural style and layout, which did not suit recreational purposes. Thus emperors of different generations gave orders for the construction of gardens at several sites in the Beijing area and spent fabulous amounts of money and manpower on them.

In addition to the Imperial Garden at the back of the Forbidden City, the gardens for enjoyment by the royal family included the Prospect Hill, once also known as His Majesty's Hill, the Beihai (North Sea), the Zhongnanhai (Central Sea and South Sea), the Garden of Good Health and Harmony, better known as the Summer Palace, the Yuanmingyuan (Garden of Perfect Splendour) which was burnt down by the allied forces of Great Britain and France during their invasion of Beijing in 1860, and the Enjoy-the-Spring Garden which also lies in ruins. All the well-preserved ones have become parks today. The Beijing Zoo used to be a garden owned by a prince of the Qing Dynasty and later became a royal garden. The Fragrant Hills Park was first named the Garden of Congenial Tranquility as one of the five gardens of the Qing Dynasty, the other four being the Garden of Light and Tranquility, the Garden of Perfect Splendour, the Enjoy-the-Spring Garden and the Summer Palace (originally the Garden of Clear Ripples).

　　紫禁城雖然建築得美輪美奐，內部陳設也極盡奢華，但是，為了顯示皇權至尊，所有的宮室殿宇都建得宏偉幽深，莊嚴凝重，致使整個宮城籠罩在森嚴肅穆的氣氛中，帝后們常年居住在這裏不免感到沉悶、壓抑。因此，歷代王朝傾注了大量的財力在皇城內外營建皇家御苑，供帝王及其家族遊賞。

　　今日已成為遊覽勝地的景山、北海、中南海、頤和園和公元一八六〇年被英法聯軍焚毀的圓明園，以及已毀圮的暢春園，都是當年的皇家園林。位於西郊的北京動物園和香山公園的前身也是皇室的園圃。前者最初是清代一位親王的花園，二十世紀改作皇家動物園；後者原名靜宜園，是與靜明園、圓明園、暢春園、清漪園（頤和園的前身）齊名的清代五園之一。

The Prospect Hill to the north of the Forbidden City. The hill is 43 metres high, and there is a pavilion on each of the five summits. The Pavilion of Ten Thousand Spring Seasons on the main summit is located on the north-south axis of Beijing and can provide people with a view of the whole city.

屏立於紫禁城北面的景山。山高四十三米，五峯上各有一亭，主峯上的萬春亭位於全城的南北中軸線上，立於亭內可以眺望北京全城。

The Drum Tower as viewed from the top of Prospect Hill. The Drum Tower and the Bell Tower further to the north are both located at the northern end of Beijing's central axis.

從景山上北望鼓樓。鼓樓及其北面的鐘樓排列在全城南北中軸線的北端。

The Bell Tower in the north and the Drum Tower to its south.

鼓樓和鐘樓南北相望。

A bird's-eye view of Beihai (North Sea). The garden has a total area of over 700,000 square metres, half of which is under water. Like the Central Sea and the South Sea, the North Sea was an important imperial garden. The three were collectively referred to as the West Gardens because of their location to the west of the Forbidden City.

北海全景。北海佔地七十餘萬平方米，水面佔全園面積一半以上。北海及其南面的中海和南海均爲皇城内最重要的皇家園林，因位於紫禁城西，當時統稱爲西苑。

Jade Flower Islet is the centre of all scenic spots in North Sea Park. Emperors of successive dynasties looked at it almost like a fairyland.

瓊華島。是北海景物的中心，也是歷代帝王心目中的海上仙山。

The White Dagoba on Jade Flower Islet is 35.9 metres high and has a diameter of 14 metres at the belly. The Lamaist dagoba was built in the Tibetan style in 1651. Buddhist scriptures and relics are kept inside.

聳立在瓊華島最高處的白塔。塔高三五點九米，最大直徑爲十四米，建於一六五一年，是一座藏式喇嘛塔，內藏經卷、衣鉢等。

The towering ancient trees on the western slopes of Jade Flower Islet have created one of the Eight Views of Yanjing. It is known as "Jade Islet in Shady Springtime". The stele, erected in 1751, is inscribed with this phrase in the calligraphy of Emperor Qianlong of the Qing.

瓊華島東坡古木參天，是"燕京八景"之一，名爲"瓊島春陰"。圖爲立於綠蔭深處的"瓊島春陰"碑，碑文爲清乾隆皇帝手筆。

It is said that an ancient emperor used a bronze dish to collect the dew from heaven, mixed it with chips of jade, and swallowed them as an elixir of life. Emperor Qianlong of the Qing didn't seek immortality by the same method. Inspired by the story, however, he had this ornamental column erected with a bronze dish on top to adorn the scenery halfway up the northern slopes of Jade Flower Islet.

銅仙承露。在瓊島北側的山腰間。據說漢武帝爲求長生不老，曾建承露盤收集露水，調和玉屑服用。乾隆皇帝據此傳說仿建，用來裝點景色。

Built in 1756, the Nine-Dragon Wall on the northern bank of North Sea is five metres high, 23 metres long, and 1.2 metres thick. It is composed of 424 seven-colour glazed bricks in bas-relief. There are nine coiling dragons on either side of the wall. There are also big and small patterns of dragons in different postures decorating the two ends and the eaves, making a total of 635.

湖北岸的九龍壁。建於一七五六年，高五米，厚一點二米，長二十七米，用四百二十四塊七色琉璃浮雕磚砌成。壁的兩面各有九條蟠龍，兩側和檐脊也都雕有大小、形態不同的龍，據統計共有龍六百三十五條。

Located on the northern bank of North Sea, the Five Dragon Pavilions overlook the Jade Flower Islet across the lake. This was the place where the emperor and empress went fishing, enjoyed the moon or watched fireworks. The pavilions are linked by stone bridges.

五龍亭。位於湖的北岸，與瓊島隔湖相望。是帝后釣魚、賞月、觀焰火的地方。各亭之間有石橋曲折相連。

The Round City after a snow viewed from the Jade Flower Islet.

With an area of 4,500 square metres, it used to be an islet in the lake. The Hall for Receiving the Light at the centre of the Round City houses a 1.5-metre-high jade Buddha statue.

從瓊華島上南望雪後的團城。團城原是湖中的一座小島，面積四千五百平方米。城中央的承光殿內供奉一尊高約一點五米的白玉佛，是京僧明寬於光緒二十四年（一八九八年）從緬甸募化來獻給慈禧太后，移供於此的。

There is a unique building by the water on the northern side of Jade Flower Islet. Looking like a crescent moon, the Extended Pavilion is two-storeyed and 300 metres long.

瓊華島北面臨水處的延樓遊廊，是園中別具一格的建築。遊廊共兩層，長三百米，呈半圓形。

Built on the northeast bank of North Sea in 1757, the Tranquil Heart Studio used to be the place where the crown princes of the Qing Dynasty received their schooling. With delicate chambers and pavilions, bridges and corridors, it seems to be a garden by itself.

静心齋。位於湖的東北岸，建於一七五七年，是北海的"園中之園"，曾是清代皇太子讀書的地方。園內橋、廊、亭、榭佈局嚴謹、構築精巧。

The Central Sea and the South Sea are separated from the North Sea only by a bridge.

與北海僅一橋之隔的中南海。

The Summer Palace with its beautiful hills and lakes. It was first named the Garden of Clear Ripples, which was burnt down by the allied forces of Great Britain and France in 1860. Reconstruction started 25 years later and was completed in 1895, and the name was changed to Yiheyuan (Garden of Good Health and Harmony). The design gives prominence to the Longevity Hill and the Kunming Lake. The total area is 290 hectares, and the buildings are measured in over 3,000 bays.

湖山相映的頤和園。一八六〇年英、法聯軍侵入北京，縱火焚毀了清漪園。二十五年後，清政府動工修復，歷時十年，至一八九五年完工，改名頤和園。全園由萬壽山、昆明湖組成，佔地二百九十公頃，宮殿園林建築三千餘間。

The East Palace Gate is the main entrance of the Garden of Good Health and Harmony, generally known as the Summer Palace. Fifteen kilometres from the urban districts of Beijing, the Summer Palace was built in the middle of the 18th century on the basis of the previous Garden of Clear Ripples.

頤和園正門——東宮門。頤和園距市中心約十五公里，建於十八世紀中葉，其前身爲清漪園。

The layout of halls and towers on the Longevity Hill suits the terrain and shows both order and variety, as one can see from this aerial photograph.

從空中俯視萬壽山，祇見殿閣樓亭依山勢排列，嚴謹中又富有變化。

Looking south from the Longevity Hill, one feels as if the Seventeen-Arch Bridge and the South Lake Islet were floating on the Kunming Lake.

自萬壽山上南望，十七孔橋和南湖島猶如浮於昆明湖上。

Looking like a rainbow, the Seventeen-Arch Bridge is eight metres wide and 150 metres long and links the East Causeway with the South Lake Islet on Kunming Lake.

連接昆明湖東堤和南湖島的十七孔橋，長一百五十米，寬八米，形若長虹。

As a symbol of successful flood control, this bronze buffalo by the Kunming Lake was cast in 1755. Inscribed on its back is a "Eulogy of the Golden Buffalo" written by the Qing Emperor Qianlong in the ancient seal style.

昆明湖畔的鎮水銅牛鑄於一七五五年，背上鑄有八十字的篆書銘文。

Skirting the northern bank of Kunming Lake, the Long Corridor extends over 728 metres and is decorated with more than 8,000 paintings of landscapes, flowers and human figures.

環繞昆明湖北岸的長廊，全長七百二十八米，廊的樑枋上繪有八千多幅山水、花卉、人物彩畫。

A phony business street was laid out along the Rear Lake in Summer Palace in the style of a market place along a lake or river in South China. Whenever the emperor and empress went there, the eunuchs would amuse them by acting like shop assistants, hawkers or customers.

後湖沿岸的買賣街，仿照江南水鄉臨河街市的格局建造，帝后常泛舟遊逛，店伙由太監充任。

There used to be a magnificent tower in Tibetan style, called Buddha's Residence Tower, in the Rear Hill area of Summer Palace. It was burnt down by the allied forces of Great Britain and France in 1860 but has been rebuilt in recent years.

萬壽山後山的香岩宗印之閣是一座宏偉的藏式寺廟。一八六〇年被英、法聯軍焚毀，近年重新修復。

The Buddha's Residence Tower is surrounded by pagodas. On the right is the Treasurehouse Pagoda of Glazed Tiles built in the 18th century. On the left is a Lamaist pagoda which has been renovated only recently.

香岩宗印之閣四周塔臺林立。圖右為五彩琉璃多寶塔，是十八世紀時的遺物。圖左為新修復的喇嘛塔。

The Garden of Harmonious Interest after a snow. Located by the eastern slope of Longevity Hill, it is an imitation of the Garden of Reserved Delight in Wuxi, Jiangsu Province. The emperor and empress used to go fishing or enjoy lotus flowers in this garden of the South China style.

雪後諧趣園。園在萬壽山東麓，仿江蘇無錫寄暢園建造，具有江南園林的特色，爲帝后觀荷垂釣之處。

Built of marble and white stone, the Jade Belt Bridge has a high arch and is one of the six bridges on the West Causeway on Kunming Lake.

昆明湖西堤的六橋之一玉帶橋。拱形的橋身、橋欄用青白石和漢白玉雕砌，宛如玉帶。

圜鳥之時盛園明圓

Plan of the three-in-one garden, with the Garden of Ten Thousand Spring Seasons in the front, the Garden of Perfect Splendour on the left, and the Garden of Eternal Spring on the right.

圓明園三園鳥瞰圖。三園分別有垣牆相隔：前為萬春園，後面並列的兩園，左為圓明園，右為長春園。

The Ten-Thousand-Flower Labyrinth, one of the scenes in the Garden of Perfect Splendour, has been reconstructed. It is a maze of winding paths between low walls in the eastern part of the garden.

新近修復的圓明園一景萬花陣。位於園的東北部，由無數迴環曲折的矮牆組成，人行其間，縱橫阻隔，難於找到出口，所以也叫迷宮。

The ruins of the Garden of Perfect Splendour (Yuanmingyuan). Located to the east of Summer Palace, it was a combination of three gardens—the Garden of Perfect Splendour, the Garden of Eternal Spring and the Garden of Ten Thousand Spring Seasons. Construction started in 1709 and was completed after more than 150 years. With an area of over 340 hectares and a building space of more than 160,000 square metres, the three-in-one garden was considered a masterpiece of Chinese gardening. In 1860, however, the allied forces of Great Britain and France reduced it to cinders.

圓明園遺跡。圓明園在頤和園之東，由圓明、長春、萬春三園組成。於一七〇九年開始興建，歷時一百五十多年始基本建成。三園佔地三百四十餘公頃，建築面積十六餘萬平方米，造園藝術堪稱世界之最，被譽爲"萬園之園"，可惜於一八六〇年焚於英法聯軍罪惡的一炬。

Ruins of the Garden of Light and Tranquility in the Jade Spring Hill. Located to the west of Kunming Lake, the garden was one of the Three Hills and Five Gardens developed in the Qing Dynasty, but was destroyed during successive wars. There used to be 16 scenic spots in the garden, but now only one remains, known as "the shadow of a pagoda on the Jade Peak".

玉泉山静明園遺址。在昆明湖迤西，爲清代所建的三山五園之一。由於歷經兵火，園已毀圮，原有的十六處景點如今祇剩"玉峯塔影"一景。

The Miaogao Pagodas on a hill north of the Jade Peak Pagoda.

玉峯塔北面山峯上的妙高塔。

Located 20 kilometres to the northwest of Beijing's urban districts, the Fragrant Hills Park has an area of 140 hectares. With thick woods, strange-looking cliffs and plenty of streams and brooks, the site was developed as the Garden of Congenial Tranquility during the Qing Dynasty. The leaves of the smoke trees on the hills turn red in late autumn.

香山公園。其前身爲静宜園，位於北京西北二十公里處，總面積約一百四十公頃。園內山奇林茂，多湧泉溪流，有"山林公園"之稱。每逢深秋，遍山黃櫨樹葉經霜變紅，構成"層林盡染"的香山秋色。

The pagoda of glazed tiles in the Temple of Clarity in the Fragrant Hills Park. The temple was built for the accommodation of the Sixth Panchen Lama who came from Tibet to Beijing to see the Qing emperor in 1780.

香山公園昭廟内的琉璃塔。昭廟是一七八〇年清政府爲接待西藏班禪來京朝見皇帝而建。

Built in 1522, the **Retreat** for Revealing One's Mind in the northeast section of the Fragrant Hills Park is a circular courtyard modelled on those south of the Yangtze River. One picture shows the chambers and pavilions in the courtyard; the other is a look from the outside.

香山公園東北部的見心齋，初建於一五二二年，是一座具有江南風格的圓形庭院。上圖爲院内的軒榭。下圖爲外觀。

The Grand View Garden, one of the places where the story of a classical Chinese novel is said to have taken place, has been simulated in Beijing through research and imagination. The famous 18th-century novel, *A Dream of Red Mansions*, has 120 chapters. The first 80 chapters were written by Cao Xueqin. The rest 40 chapters are believed to have been written by Gao E, although there are still controversies on the authorship. The novel describes the vicissitudes of the aristocratic Jia family, focussing on the tragic love story of the young man Jia Baoyu and young woman Lin Daiyu. The Grand View Garden was built specially for the home visit of Jia Yuanchun, eldest daughter of the Jia family serving as an imperial consort in the palace. After she returned to the palace, her brothers, sisters and cousins moved into the chambers and courtyards of the Grand View Garden, which thus became the scenes of a great many events in the novel. Construction of a simulated version of the garden started in 1982 and was completed in 1987. Located in the southwest corner of urban Beijing, the garden has an area of over 12 hectares and more than 40 scenic spots. The layout, architecture, and arrangement of hills and streams, flowers and trees are all based on descriptions in the novel. The picture shows a body of lake water in the garden.

位於北京城區西南隅的大觀園，爲一新建的仿古園林。一九八二年開始興建，一九八七年建成，佔地十二多公頃。大觀園原是成書於十八世紀的著名小説《紅樓夢》所描繪的一座園林。《紅樓夢》共一百二十回，曹雪芹著（據傳後四十回爲高鶚續補）。全書以貴族青年賈寶玉、林黛玉的愛情悲劇爲主線，描寫貴族世家賈家由盛而衰的過程。大觀園是賈府長女元春晉封爲貴妃回府省親時建的，而後其弟及姐妹進園居住，於是大觀園成爲展現小説故事的主要場景之一。現建的大觀園共有景點四十餘處，園内結構、佈局、山水花木的配置等全以《紅樓夢》所描繪的爲藍本。圖爲該園中部的一泓湖水。

Altars, Temples and Mausoleums

祭壇　寺廟　陵墓

Most of the altars and temples, including the Ancestral Temple of the royal family, the Altar of Land and Grain, the Temple of Heaven, the Temple of Earth, the Altar of the Sun and the Altar of the Moon, date to the 15th century.

All through the dynasties, the emperors appealed to religion to seek longevity or the eternity of their throne. They subscribed to Buddhism or Taoism or both. Large sums were allocated from the state treasury for the construction of temples for the various sects of the Buddhist or Taoist faith. The temples and pagodas remaining today show a great variety of styles, and some of them are considered masterpieces of traditional architecture.

Three mortuary complexes lie in the hills to the northwest, southwest and east of Beijing. They consist of the tombs of 22 emperors of the Ming and Qing dynasties and their empresses and consorts. As soon as an emperor ascended the throne, he would give the order for the construction of his tomb, which would take several years or even a few decades to complete and cost tremendous amounts of human and material resources.

祭壇、寺廟和古陵幽宮在北京古跡中最富有神幻色彩。它們給古城增添了奇異的風采。

帝王祭祀祖先的太廟和祭祀天、地、日、月、土地、五穀等神靈的祭壇，大都建於十五世紀。這些建築依照傳統規制建成，造型獨特。

歷代帝王爲求得福壽綿長、皇位永繼，往往借助於宗教的力量，或提倡佛法，或尊奉道教，興建各種教派的寺廟。這些宗教的建築風格，各具特色，有的堪稱古建築中的精華。

北京的西北、西南和東面的山山嶺嶺之間分佈着三個陵墓羣，共埋葬着明、清兩代二十二個帝王及其后妃。這一座座陵墓大都在帝王初登皇位時便開始營建，歷時幾年、十幾年乃至幾十年方竣工。

Located in the southern part of Beijing, the Temple of Heaven was built in 1420. Emperors of the Ming and Qing dynasties came here to pray for a good harvest in spring and for rain in summer, and to offer sacrifices to heaven in winter. In line with the ancient Chinese concept of a round heaven and a square earth, the buildings in the temple were given a circular shape, except the double wall, which is circular in the north but square in the south, and the outer walls of the Altar of Heaven and the Hall of Prayer for Good Harvest, which are square.

天壇。位於城南，始建於一四二○年，是明清兩代帝王春季祈穀，夏至祈雨，冬至祈天的地方。遵循"天圓地方"的説法，這裏的建築多呈圓形。唯兩重壇牆北圓南方，圜丘壇和祈年殿的外沿圍牆呈方形。

Built in 1420, the Hall of Prayer for Good Harvest in the Temple of Heaven is 38 metres high and has a diameter of 32 metres. Early in spring the emperor would come here to pray for a good harvest later in the year.

天壇祈年殿。始建於一四二〇年，殿高三十八米，直徑三十二米。每年初春皇帝在此祈禱五穀豐登。

Coffered ceiling in the Hall of Prayer for Good Harvest. With three layers of eaves, the hall is supported by four pillars in the middle, representing the four seasons. Two outer rings of 12 pillars each symbolize the 12 months and the 12 two-hour periods in a cycle of day and night.

祈年殿藻井。大殿的三重檐由二十八根巨柱支撐着，中央四柱代表一年四季，外圍兩圈各十二根，分別代表一年十二個月和一天十二個時辰。

Built in 1530, the Echo Wall in the Temple of Heaven is a circular structure composed of polished bricks on the inside. A whisper at one point of the wall can be heard at any other point.

天壇迴音壁。建於一五三〇年，爲一圓形的垣牆，因內側牆面平整光滑，內弧規準，附之說話，聲音可迅速傳到牆體各部位。

The Altar of Heaven, where the emperors offered sacrifices to heaven, was built in 1530. The three-tiered altar is five metres high. The steps and railings on each tier were constructed in nines or multiples of nine, which is the numerical representation of *yang* (the masculine or the positive) in the *yin-yang* theory. Traditionally heaven is considered masculine or positive, while earth is believed to be feminine or negative.

圜丘壇，帝王祭天的聖壇，建於一五三〇年。壇高五米，分三層，各層欄板、望柱及臺階數目均爲九或九的倍數，以符"九重天"之説。

Built in 1530, the Temple of Earth in the northern part of Beijing has square altars and walls in line with the ancient Chinese concept of a square earth. The high terrace on the left is the Altar of Earth, while the two square stone terraces on the right represent the country's great mountains and rivers respectively, as indicated by the carvings on them

位於城北的地壇建於一五三○年，它的垣牆、祭壇都呈方形。圖左的高臺是地壇，右面的兩方石座分別爲象徵五嶽和四瀆的山石座和水石座。

The observatory inside Jianguomen (Gate of National Reconstruction) was built in 1279. Of the 15 astronomical instruments originally kept there, seven were moved to the Zijinshan (Purple Gold Mountain) Observatory in Nanjing in 1931. The eight instruments remaining here were manufactured in the 17th and 18th centuries.

矗立在建國門内的古觀象臺始建於一二七九年。臺上原有古代天文儀器十五件，其中的七件於一九三一年遷至南京紫金山天文臺，現陳列的八件是十七和十八世紀時鑄造的。

Located in the Western Hills 35 kilometres from Beijing's urban districts, the Ordination Terrace Temple was built more than 1,300 years ago.

座落在西山深處的戒臺寺．距市區三十五公里．是建於一千三百多年前的古剎。

The Ordination Terrace in the temple bearing the same name has three tiers and is several metres high. It was built in the 11th century by the high priest Fa Jun who presided over ceremonies there for novices to pledge to observe monastic commandments. It is the biggest terrace for the purpose in China.

戒臺寺內的戒臺是中國最大的一座．臺分三級．高數米。爲十一世紀時．僧法均在寺內開壇傳戒而修建的。

Located eight kilometres north of the Ordination Terrace Temple, the Temple of the Pool and Wild Mulberries was built more than 1,600 years ago. It is the oldest temple remaining in Beijing. There are 72 pagodas built in the Jin (Jurchen), Yuan, Ming or Qing dynasties in the woods at the front of the temple. Their different styles provide valuable data for a study of Buddhist architecture in China.

潭柘寺在戒臺寺以北八公里處。該寺建於一千六百多年前，是北京最古老的寺廟。寺前樹木葱蘢，樹間有金、元、明、清的僧塔七十二座，造型各異，對研究中國佛教建築極有價值。

The Thunder Cave in the hills southwest of Beijing, where Buddhist scriptures were engraved on rocks in nine caves from the 7th century onward. In the Thunder Cave, which is the No.5 cave, the scriptures are found on the four walls, and more than a thousand Buddha statues are carved on four octagonal stone pillars, which are known as A-Thousand-Buddha Pillars. Two relics of Buddha placed in the cave in the year 616 were discovered in November 1981.

石經山中的雷音洞。石經山在北京西南郊，山中的九個石窟內珍藏着自公元七世紀以來歷代雕刻的石經版。雷音洞爲第五窟，窟內四壁皆嵌有經版；四根八棱形石柱上雕着千餘尊佛像，稱爲千佛柱。一九八一年十一月在雷音洞內還發現公元六一六年放置的兩粒佛舍利。

A copy of the Murals of Buddha and of gods in the Temple of the
Sea of Dharma, built in 1443 at the southern foot of Cuiwei
Mountain west of Beijing.

法海寺壁畫。法海寺位於北京西郊翠微山麓，建成於一四四三年。因寺
內繪有技藝精湛的巨型壁畫而稱譽京都。

The Temple of Azure Clouds at the estern foot of Fragrant Hills was built in 1289. With an area of four hectares, it is known for a hall of the statues of 508 arhats, the Sun Yat-sen Memorial Hall, and diamond throne pagodas.

香山東麓的碧雲寺。初建於一二八九年，佔地四公頃，是西山風景區中最崇麗的一座寺院。寺內有供奉着五百零八尊佛像的羅漢堂、孫中山紀念堂和金剛寶座塔等勝跡。

Pagodas are found in Beijing's many temples, showing the architectural styles of different periods and schools. In addition to those presented earlier in this album, here are a few more:

1 The stupa for the enshrinement of Buddha relics in the Dwelling-in-the-Clouds Temple. It was built in the Liao Dynasty almost 1,000 years ago.

2 The White Dagoba in the Temple of Divine Respense in an urban district of Beijing. It was designed and built with the help of a Nepalese architect in 1271.

3 and 4 The five Diamond Throne Pagodas in the Temple of True Awakening, located along the Changhe (Long River) outside Beijing's Xizhimen (Straight West Gate). The five pagodas rest on a 7.7-metre-high base with carvings of images of Buddha, words in Sanskrit and ornamental designs.

5 The pagoda in the Temple of Benevolence and Longevity at Balizhuang (Eight-Li Village) in Beijing's west suburbs. Built in 1576, the pagoda has concentrated eaves typical of a pagoda of the Ming Dynasty.

6 The Silver Hill Pagodas in the Silver Hills in Changping northwest of Beijing. Early in the 12th century there were as many as 72 Buddhist monasteries and nunneries in and around the Silver Hills, and the largest of them was called the Splendour of Dharma Temple. The picture shows pagodas in the temple, built in memory of the high priests of different periods.

北京多寺廟，幾乎凡寺皆有塔，這些塔建築時代不同，造型、風格殊異。這裏僅展示幾座頗有特色的。

1 高三十米的雲居寺舍利塔，是距今近千年的遼代建築。

2 屹立於市區的妙應寺白塔，建於一二七一年，是尼泊爾工匠的傑作。

3、4 西直門外長河畔的真覺寺金剛寶座塔。五座尖塔矗立在高七點七米的塔基上，塔基周圍雕刻有佛像、梵文和紋飾。

5 西郊八里莊的慈壽寺塔建於一五七六年，是明代密檐塔的代表作。

6 深藏在北京西北昌平銀山中的古塔羣。十二世紀初葉，銀山上下有寺院七十二座，古塔羣是最大的一座寺院法華寺的歷代高僧墓塔。

1

2

3

6

4

5

Located close to the Temple of Azure Clouds, the Temple of the Reclining Buddha was built at the turn of the 7th century. The bronze statue of Buddha, cast in 1321, shows Sakyamuni giving his last instructions to 12 disciples on his deathbed. It is five metres long and weighs 54 tons. The other picture shows the archway covered with glazed tiles in front of the temple.

與碧雲寺相鄰的卧佛寺，始建於七世紀初。寺內的這尊銅佛長五米，重五十四噸，鑄於一三二一年，表現釋迦牟尼涅槃時囑咐弟子的神態。左圖為卧佛寺山門前的琉璃牌坊。

The Lamasery of Harmony and Peace, the largest lamasery in Beijing, is located in the northern part of the city. It was the residence of Emperor Yongzheng (r. 1723-35) of the Qing Dynasty before his enthronement, and was converted into a lamasery in 1744. The picture on the left shows the name of the lamasery written in the Manchu, Han, Tibetan and Mongolian scripts.

雍和宮是北京最大的一座喇嘛廟，位於城區北部，原是清雍正帝（一七二三——一七三五年在位）即位前的藩邸。一七四四年改爲喇嘛廟。圖爲用滿、漢、藏、蒙四種文字書寫的雍和宮匾額。

The Hall of the Dharma Wheel, one of the five main halls in the Lamasery of Harmony and Peace, is used for major religious ceremonies.

雍和宮五大殿之一法輪殿，是喇嘛舉行隆重宗教儀式的地方。

Lamas studying Buddhist scriptures in a hall of the Lamasery of Harmony and Peace.

雍和宮的喇嘛們在學習經文。

A standing statue of Maitreya in the Tower of Infinite Happiness in the Lamasery of Harmony and Peace is 18 metres high and three metres in diameter. Carved from a single trunk of white sandalwood, it was presented to the Qing government by the Seventh Panchen Lama in 1750 in appreciation of the suppression of a rebellion by its troops.

雍和宮萬福閣内的彌勒立像，像高十八米、直徑三米，用整棵的白檀香木雕成。這棵白檀木是一七五〇年西藏第七世喇嘛爲感謝清政府派兵平叛，贈送的禮品。

The Avatamsaka Bell in the Temple of Awakening in Beijing's west suburbs is one of the largest bells of the world. It is 6.75 metres high, has an outer rim 3.3 metres in diameter, and weighs 46.5 tons. Buddhist sutras totalling 227,000 characters are inscribed on both sides of the bell. Cast early in the 15th century, the bell tolls in deep, vigorous tones and can be heard dozens of kilometres away. On the right is a picture of the bell tower.

西郊覺生寺內的華嚴鐘是世界巨鐘之一．鑄於十五世紀初。鐘身通高六點七五米，口沿外徑三點三米，重四六點五噸。鐘身內外鑄有佛教經咒共約二十二萬七千字。鐘聲深沉宏亮，擊之數十里可聞。右圖爲鐘樓外景。

The White Cloud Temple outside Beijing's Xibianmen (West Informal Gate) is the best-known Taoist temple in the city. The Taoist religion appeared in China in the 2nd century, and the White Cloud Temple was first built in the 8th century when the religion began to flourish.

When the religion began to flourish. The pictures show the arch way in front of the temple and the interior of the Hall of the Jade Emperor.

西便門外的白雲觀是北京著名的道觀，建於八世紀。圖爲觀前的牌樓和玉皇殿內景。

There are followers of different religions in Beijing, including quite a number of Moslems. The picture shows the interior of the mosque on Ox Street, where most of the residents are moslems.

北京自古是一個多民族聚居的城市，由於各族宗教信仰不同，城内城外建有各種教派的寺廟。這是回民聚居區的牛街清真寺内景。

The Xishiku Cathedral viewed from the inside and the outside. Built in 1890, it used to be one of the four cathedrals in Beijing.

西什庫教堂的內景和外觀。教堂建於一八九〇年，曾是北京的四大天主教堂之一。

The Thirteen Tombs of the Ming Dynasty are located in the hills 50 kilometres to the northwest of Beijing. Construction of the tombs started in 1409 and ended with the fall of the Ming Dynasty in 1644. In over 200 years tombs were built over an area of 40 square kilometres, **which is surrounded by walls totalling 40 kilometres. Each tomb** is located at the foot of a separate hill and is linked with the other tombs by a road called the Sacred Way. The stone archway at the southern end of the Sacred Way, built in 1540, is 14 metres high and 29 metres wide, and is decorated with designs of clouds, waves and divine animals.

明十三陵位於北京西北郊的羣山中、距市區五十公里。陵園面積四十平方公里、外圍築有四十公里的城垣。從一四〇九年興築第一座陵墓起、至一六四四年明朝滅亡、這項工程延續了二百餘年。十三座陵各踞一山之下、中有神路貫通。圖爲十三陵神路南端的石牌坊、建於一五四〇年、面闊二十九米、高十四米、結構宏偉。夾柱石和額枋上雕有飛雲、湧浪和各種神獸圖案。

The Sacred Way inside the gate of the Ming Tombs is lined with 18 pairs of stone human figures and animals. These include four each of three types of officials: civil, military and meritorious officials, symbolizing those who assist the emperor in the administration of the state, plus four each of six types of animals: lion, griffin, camel, elephant, unicorn and horse.

陵園大門内的神路兩旁分列着十八對石人石獸。石人有文、武、勳臣三種、象徵輔佐皇帝的文武百官。石獸有獅、獬豸、駱駝、象、麒麟、馬六種。

The soul tower of Changling, which is the tomb of emperor Chengzu, the third emperor of the Ming Dynasty whose personal name was Zhu Di, and of his empress. Built in 1413, the mausoleum extends over an area of 100,000 square metres. The soul tower, which tells people whose tomb it is, rests on a circular wall called the "city of treasures" which surrounds the burial mound. The "city of treasures" at Changling has a length of more than a kilometre.

長陵明樓。長陵是明代第三個皇帝明成祖朱棣及其皇后的陵墓，建成於一四一三年，佔地約十萬平方米。明樓是陵墓的標誌，建在寶城上，寶城内即是墳丘。長陵的寶城周長約一公里餘。

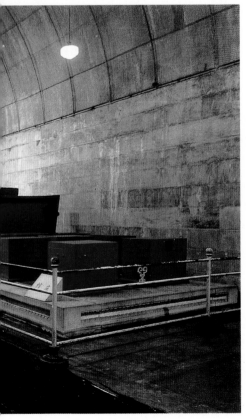

The underground palace at Dingling, the tomb of Emperor Shenzong, the 13th emperor of the Ming Dynasty, whose personal name was Zhu Yijun, and of his two empresses. The tomb was completed in 1590, but it was not excavated until the 1950s. In 1959 the site was officially designated as the Dingling Museum. The underground palace consists of an antechamber, a central chamber and a rear chamber plus the left and right annexes. One of the pictures shows the central chamber where the sacrificial utensils are on display, and the other, the rear chamber where the coffins are placed.

定陵地下宮殿。定陵是明代第十三個皇帝朱翊鈞及其兩位皇后的陵墓，建成於一五九〇年。定陵的地宮於本世紀五十年代發掘，一九五九年正式闢爲定陵博物館。地宮由前、中、後三殿和左、右配殿組成。圖爲陳設祭器的中殿和放置棺槨的後殿。

The Eastern Tombs of the Qing Dynasty in the hills 125 kilometres northeast of Beijing. Buried here are five emperors, 15 empresses and over 100 imperial consorts of the Qing. The Eastern Tombs and the Western Tombs are the two mortuary complexes of the Qing Dynasty near Beijing.

清代皇陵有兩處——東陵和西陵。圖爲東陵陵區，位於北京東北一百二十五公里處。在這片岡巒環抱的原野上，埋葬着清代的五帝、十五后和一百多個妃嬪。

The Sacred Way at
the Eastern Tombs.

清東陵神路。

The Western Tombs of the Qing Dynasty 120 kilometres south-west of Beijing, with a periphery of more than 100 kilometres, is a complex of the tombs of four emperors, three empresses, three imperial consorts and four princes and princesses.

北京西南一百二十多公里處的西陵，是清代的又一處陵園。這裏有帝陵四座，皇后陵三座，妃園寢三座，王公、公主園寢四座。

Tailing at the centre of the Western Tombs is the burial site of
Emperor Yongzheng of the Qing Dynasty (r. 1723-35), his empress,
and one of his consorts.

位於西陵中心的泰陵，這裏埋葬着清雍正皇帝和他的一位皇后和一位皇
貴妃。

The Great Wall

長　城

To the northwest and north of Beijing, a huge, serrated wall zigzags its way to the east and west along the undulating mountains. This is the Great Wall, which is said to be visible from the moon.

Construction of the Great Wall started in the 7th century B.C. The vassal states under the Zhou Dynasty in the northern parts of the country each built their own walls for defence purposes. After the state of Qin unified China in 221 B.C., it joined the walls to hold off the invaders from the Xiongnu tribes in the north and extended them to more than 10,000 *li* or 5,000 kilometres. This is the origin of the name of the "10,000-*li* Great Wall."

The Great Wall was renovated from time to time after the Qin Dynasty. A major renovation started with the founding of the Ming Dynasty in 1368, and took 200 years to complete. The wall we see today is almost exactly the result of this effort. With a total length of over 6,000 kilometres, it extends to the Jiayu Pass in Gansu Province in the west and to the mouth of the Yalu River in Liaoning Province in the east. What lies north of Beijing is but a small section of it.

在北京西北和北面連綿的羣山中，一道鋸齒形的高牆隨山勢起伏蜿蜒，向東西方向延伸，不見首尾。這便是據說在月球上可以看到的長城。

長城的修築可上溯到公元前七世紀。當時割據一方的諸侯國爲了防守，在自己的領土上修築城牆。公元前二二一年秦國統一了中國，爲防禦北方的匈奴貴族南擾，將原來北方三個諸侯國的長城加以連貫修葺並延至一萬多里（兩里爲一公里），"萬里長城"因而得名。秦以後的一些朝代對長城也曾屢加修建。最後一次大規模修築始於明代建國之初的一三六八年，全部工程歷時二百年纔完成。修成後的明長城西至甘肅嘉峪關，東至遼寧鴨綠江口，全長六千多公里。今天逶迤於北京北部的長城就是它的一段。

The Badaling section of the Great Wall snaking along the
mountains northwest of Beijing was built at the beginning of the
Ming Dynasty in the 14th century. Being 7.8 metres high and
5.8 metres wide at the top on the average, it has battle forts at
important points, including the corners.

蜿蜒於北京西北羣山中的八達嶺長城。這一帶長城始建於十四世紀
明王朝建立之初。城牆平均高七點八米，牆頂平均寬五點八米，在
城牆轉角或險要處建有高聳的敵臺。

The Badaling section of
the Great Wall in autumn.

八達嶺長城之秋。

Cloud Terrace (Yuntai) at the Pass of Conscripted Labourers (Juyongguan). Located 10 kilometres south of the Badaling section of the Great Wall and built in an 18.5-kilometre-long valley, the pass has always been an important gateway northwest of Beijing. The name is believed to have its origin in the workers and slaves conscripted to build the Great Wall in ancient times. Cloud Terrace, built in 1345, was originally the base of a pagoda overlooking the main road of the town of the pass. The arched gate of the terrace and the walls inside the arch are decorated with carvings of elephants, lions, birds, flowers and heavenly kings as well as charms in six languages—Sanskrit, Tibetan, Phatspa (Mongolian), Uygur, West Xia and Han. The one of the lower pictures shows part of the carvings inside the arch.

居庸關及雲臺。居庸關是古代北京西北面的重要關隘，位於八達嶺以南十公里處，建在一條長十八公里餘的溪谷中。雲臺是居庸關關城內一座過街塔的基座，建於元代。基座的券門上和券洞內刻有鳥獸花草圖案、天王佛像和用六種文字題刻的經咒等。

The Mutianyu section of the Great Wall, 70 kilometres northeast of Beijing, is linked to the Gubeikou section on the east and the Badaling section on the west. it is one of the best sections of the Great Wall.

慕田峪長城。位於北京東北七十公里處，東、西分別與古北口、八達嶺長城相連接，亦爲明代所建。

Battle forts built on the summits of hills.

建於峯巔的敵臺

The Mutianyu section of the Great Wall is crenelatted for watching and shooting at the invading enemy. Some of the battle forts on the wall are as close as 50 metres apart.

慕田峪長城的兩側都築有供瞭望、射擊的垛口，城上敵臺林立，相距最近的不足五十米。

Located in Miyun County northeast of Beijing, the Jinshanling division of the Great Wall, like the Simatai division, belongs to the Gubeikou section of the colossal defence barrier.

氣勢宏偉的金山嶺長城。這段長城位於北京東北的密雲縣境內，因這一帶地形復雜，所以城上建有多種防禦設施。

The battlements in the Jinshanling division of the Great Wall are built along the ridge of a mountain, where the soldiers can resist the invading enemy by taking advantage of the high terrain.

沿山脊而建的戰牆，士兵可在牆後居高臨下禦敵。

A decrepit battle fort at dusk often reminds one of the battles in ancient times.

夕陽中殘破的敵臺，最容易勾起人的思古之情。

Located to the east of Jinshanling, the Simatai division of the Great Wall is 3,000 metres long and has 35 battle forts. The wall rises and falls with the precipitous mountain ridge, while the battle forts are located high up the hills.

金山嶺迤東的司馬臺長城，總長三千米，共有敵樓三十五座。城牆順着壁立的山脊起伏伸延，敵樓高聳於羣峯之上。

Sights One Shouldn't Miss

郊 野 風 光

You may have visited Beijing before and seen most of the well-known sights. But the geographical complexity of the area has given it more tourist sites or potential ones. There is an abundance of hills, rivers and ponds in the locality. Some of the landscapes combine the vigour and magnificence of North China with the elegance and delicacy of the south.

The mountains and rivers at Shidu (Ten Crossings) in the southwest suburbs are comparable to the scenery along the picturesque Lijiang River in Guilin, South China. In Yanqing County northwest of the city, the Longqing Gorge looks almost as precipitous as one of the Yangtze River Gorges. The northeast suburbs boast two unique pools, the Black Dragon Pool and the White Dragon Pool, where the water is clear and the rocks grotesque. Other attractions include the Miaofeng (Divine Summit) Mountain, the Baihua (Hundred Flowers) Mountain and the Shangfang (Upper Square) Mountain. You may also enjoy a casual walk in any of the suburbs to see a few cottages dotting the fields, a few donkeys grazing at the foot of a hill, or a whole grove of persimmons.

到北京來的旅遊者大都祇着眼於這裏的宮殿園林和聞名於世的萬里長城，而忽略了京郊那些野趣盎然的風光。

北京南臨華北大平原，背倚蒙古高原，境内河湖泉潭密佈，山水風光兼有江南明麗和北地雄渾的特色。

西南郊的十渡山水被譽爲北國的"桂林小灕江"；西北延慶縣境内的龍慶峽，曲折險峻，猶如縮小了的"長江三峽"；東北郊有水清石奇的黑龍潭和白龍潭。此外，如妙峯山、百花山、上方山等也都是絶佳去處。若漫步四野，縱然是不知名的一片柿林、數棟村舍或幾匹悠然行走在山徑間的小毛驢，也自有韻味。

With its source in the Tai-hang Mountains, the Juma River drains Fangshan County southwest of Beijing.

拒馬河景色。拒馬河發源於太行山脈，流經北京西南的房山區境內。

One of the "Ten Crossings" along the Juma River. As the river flows between precipitous cliffs in Fangshan County, it creates a relishing landscape similar to one along the Lijiang River in Guilin, South China. The site is called "Ten Crossings" because, to walk from the banks along the upper reaches of the Juma River to those in the middle reaches, one has to cross the river ten times.

被譽爲"北國桂林山水"的十渡一景。拒馬河中上游河段，穿流在陡峭如壁的峯嶺之間，兩岸景色奇麗，河道曲折。遊人沿河岸行走，從上游到中游，需十渡拒馬河，十渡即因此而得名。

Farmhouses in a hilly environment typical
of North China.

深山農舍。這裏的山雄渾粗獷，具有北國特色。

A country road.

在村道上。

A grove of
persimmons.

農家的柿林。

The Longqing Gorge in
Yanqing County northwest
of Beijing.

北京西北延慶縣境内的龍慶
峽。

The Black Dragon Pool and the White Dragon Pool in Miyun County do not look alike, although both are formed by water from mountain springs.

密雲縣境內的黑龍潭和白龍潭。兩潭皆由山泉匯集而成，但各有異趣。

Built in 1189, the Reed Gully Bridge (Marco Polo Bridge) spanning the Yongding River is the oldest stone arch bridge remaining in Beijing. Located 15 kilometres southwest of Beijing, it is 266.5 metres long and 7.5 metres wide. The balusters and ornamental pylons are decorated with 485 stone lions in a variety of sizes and postures.

横跨在永定河上的盧溝橋。橋在北京西南約十五公里處，始建於一一八九年，是北京現存最古老的石造聯拱橋。橋全長二六六點五米，寬七點五米，兩側的石欄望柱上共刻有四百八十五隻形態不同的石獅。

A stele at the eastern end of the Reed Gully Bridge is inscribed with characters meaning "Moon over the Reed Gully Bridge at Dawn" in the calligraphy of Emperor Qianlong of the Qing Dynasty. The bridge has always been an important link for land traffic between north and south. In the old days people came here to bid farewell to friends and relatives leaving Beijing.

立於橋東頭的"盧溝曉月"碑，碑文爲清乾隆皇帝手書。古代盧溝橋曾是通往南北的要道，親友出行，主人往往要送至這裏作別。

The Stone Flower Cavern in Fangshan County is a karst cavern seldom seen in North China. It is 170 metres high and over 3,000 metres long. The seven tiers of the cavern are separated from one another by a distance of a few dozen metres, but are linked by balustraded stairs. The stalagmites and stalactites in the cavern take a great variety of shapes, with some of the stalactites looking like the broad cloth banners in a Buddhist temple.

房山區境內的石花洞，是北方罕見的一處溶洞羣。溶洞高約一百七十米，共七層，各層之間相距幾十米，有扶梯相通。溶洞全長三千多米，裏面佈滿了千姿百態的石柱、石笋、石幔等。

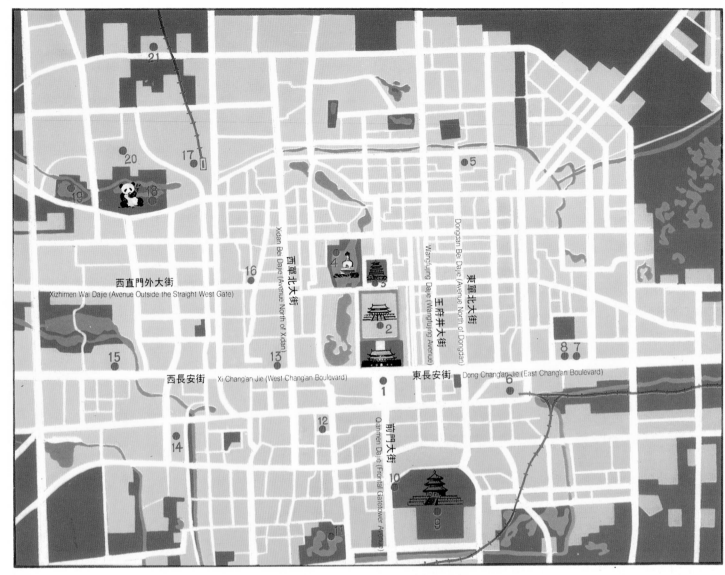

SIGHTS IN THE URBAN DISTRICTS OF BEIJING

北京市區名勝分佈圖

1. Tiananmen Square
2. Forbidden City
3. Prospect Hill Park
4. North Sea Park
5. Lamasery of Harmony and Peace
6. Beijing Railway Station
7. Friendship Store
8. International Club
9. Temple of Heaven Park
10. Beijing Museum of Natural History
11. Taoranting (Joyous Pavilion) Park
12. Grand View Garden
13. Cultural Palace of Nationalities
14. White Cloud Taoist Temple
15. Military Museum of the Chinese People's Revolution
16. White Pagoda Temple
17. Xizhimen (Straight West Gate) Railway Station
18. Beijing Zoo
19. Purple Bamboo Garden
20. Five-Pagoda Temple
21. Big Bell Temple (Temple of Awakening)

1. 天安門廣場
2. 故宮
3. 景山公園
4. 北海公園
5. 雍和宮
6. 北京火車站
7. 友誼商店
8. 國際俱樂部
9. 天壇公園
10. 自然博物館
11. 陶然亭公園
12. 大觀園
13. 民族文化宮
14. 白雲觀
15. 軍事博物館
16. 白塔寺
17. 西直門火車站
18. 北京動物園
19. 紫竹院公園
20. 五塔寺
21. 大鐘寺（覺生寺）

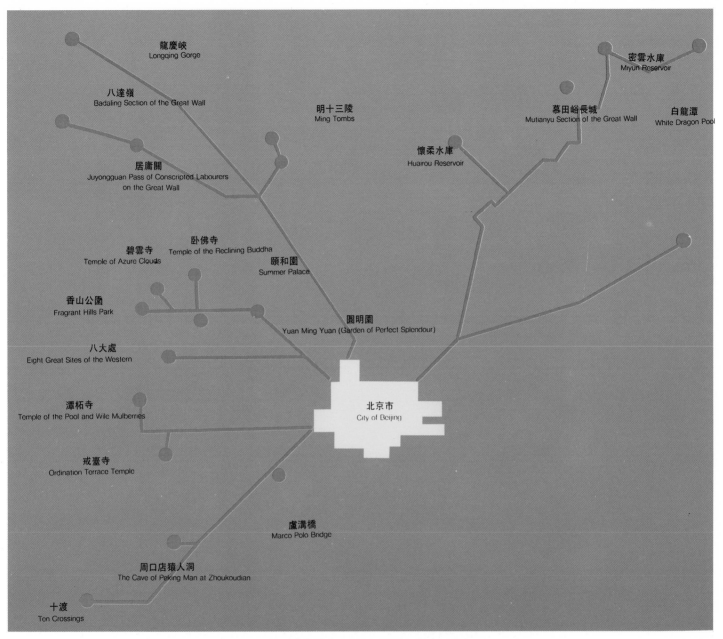

龍慶峽
Longqing Gorge

八達嶺
Badaling Section of the Great Wall

明十三陵
Ming Tombs

密雲水庫
Miyun Reservoir

慕田峪長城
Mutianyu Section of the Great Wall

白龍潭
White Dragon Pool

居庸關
Juyongguan Pass of Conscripted Labourers
on the Great Wall

懷柔水庫
Huairou Reservoir

碧雲寺
Temple of Azure Clouds

臥佛寺
Temple of the Reclining Buddha

頤和園
Summer Palace

香山公園
Fragrant Hills Park

圓明園
Yuan Ming Yuan (Garden of Perfect Splendour)

八大處
Eight Great Sites of the Western

北京市
City of Beijing

潭柘寺
Temple of the Pool and Wile Mulberries

戒臺寺
Ordination Terrace Temple

盧溝橋
Marco Polo Bridge

周口店猿人洞
The Cave of Peking Man at Zhoukoudian

十渡
Ten Crossings

SIGHTS IN THE SUBURBAN DISTRICTS OF BEIJING (SKETCH MAP)
北京郊區名勝分佈示意圖

北 京 攬 勝

廖 頻 編

*

外文出版社出版

（中國北京百萬莊路 24 號）

深圳華新彩印製版有限公司製版印刷

中國國際圖書貿易總公司發行

（中國北京車公莊西路 35 號）

北京郵政信箱第 399 號　郵政編碼 100044

1989 年第一版

1992 年第二次印刷

1993 年第三次印刷

1994 年第四次印刷

（英漢）

ISBN 7—119—00735—1 / J・575（外）

04800

85—EC—330P